The Little Guide to Leaving

Katie Glasgow-Palmer

Press

Published by 99% Press, 2023

an imprint of Lasavia Publishing Ltd.

Auckland, New Zealand

www.lasaviapublishing.com

Copyright © Katie Glasgow-Palmer, 2023

Design: Daniela Gast

ISBN: 978-1-991083-02-9

To all those who made it so hard to leave

taiao

something about the ocean's twin cadences
the rumble of distant breaks and
the delicate shy lapping where the water meets
the sand, the wind's
melodramatic heaving

primes the air for grand announcements
statements so embarrassingly life-altering
we could never say in another soundscape
not even the deathly vaccum chamber of a stationary car
or amidst the gentle murmur of a moderately busy
chinese takeaway-cum-fish and chip shop

I love you

seaglass and shells and rocks tumble slowly
pulsing rhythmically in and out, sighed by distant lungs

I'm worried about you

the sky is gentle and changeable but casts no judgement
however
walking side by side along the shore feels as obscene
as making love in public
oceanic sighs and moans ready to commiserate with
the coming tears

I'm moving away

it seems a shame our footprints vanish from the sand

Welcome Home
by Dave Dobbyn

mum advised me to listen to him on every return trip
and stare down at the mosaic of fields
and barren folds of former mountains
letting the sentimental chords
the prestigious image of a genuine powhiri
let you gently back down to earth
it always made her emotional
to be fair, I never needed any help with that

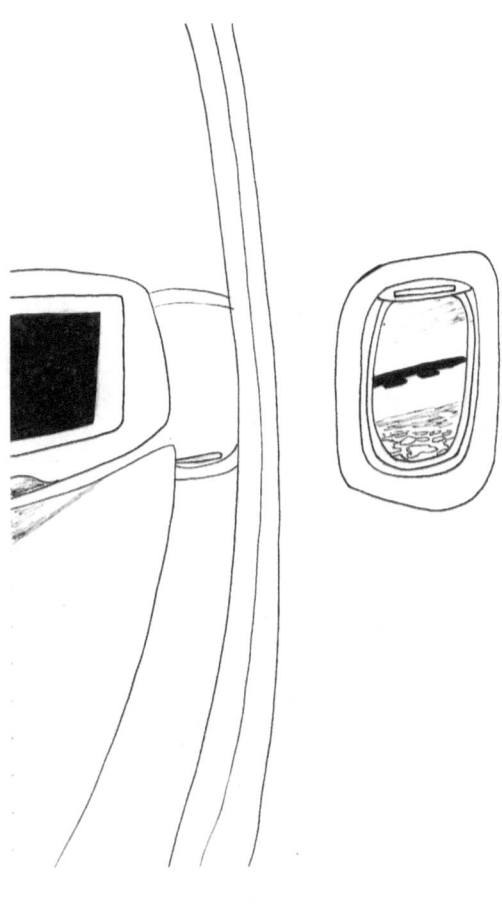

we stared up at the Southern Cross
liquid clear night

and he told me not to go

he told me I didn't know what I had
and that if I left, I would lose it

foreign

I wish someone had told me how nothing changes

and yet everything becomes smaller

locks you out

takes on a different hue

they discontinued Pods

there are more people cold on Queen Street over winter

they painted over

Tama Nui Te Ra

who raged proud and orange from the walls

of Parnell primary's assembly school hall

silver hairs make sudden appearances

and your friend doesn't host those house parties anymore

with the warm braziers and light beers

their family now lives across the city

you weren't invited for the final gathering

my hands are too soft

I am driven to my hostel
I watch landscapes pass by, land carefully
cultivated, washing hung out to dry beside small
houses with fires burning, wood from nearby forests and
small patches of vegetables, livestock huddled

my food is prepared and cooked on hand sanded
tables, we drink wine from nearby vineyards

a nurse takes my temperature, monitors my symptoms
in a hospital built and run by imported labour
I must have eaten something strange
in the oily excess of the buffet the night before

forcing a useless smile
I say thank you in what I hope is the correct language

protect your heart

be ready to leave at any time
therefore, throw wild abandon to your interactions
Chug that vodka! Kiss that stranger! Take that mystery drug!
sense the magic in a split second of eye contact
and follow its thread into his one person tent
head 2000km away on a break without telling
a soul

temporariness is a drug
even more thrilling in large countries where
bumping into people you know is
near impossible

therefore, make your life a playground, a circus
every party and mishap and missed flight and lost luggage
and fainting episode
and near miss
and traumatising terrifying encounter
nothing more than a story

geographical cure

it's cliche for a reason
it's unavoidable
no matter where you go, your heart will be split
you may never again enjoy the luxury of Crowded
House's
Everyone I love is here
but then again, you get to live a double life if you want
main character, a real life star of your own silver screen

tall poppy

it's a tired cliche
but wait, now you're a tired cliche
you must know your only option is to talk yourself down
never letting anyone in on the fact that
you're actually proud of your new life
pride is a luxury to be shared only with the very few
(or just wait til you're back overseas)

it's true, you can play your own drum
and see who sticks by you
definitely the riskier option
or you can rehearse each conversation and play it on repeat
yes, it's pretty different over there
no, I don't speak the language yet
yes, I am coming back for Christmas
no, we don't know how lucky we are
while you mind drifts above your body

you'll need to cultivate more strength than you knew you had
stay on the defense
don't let them win.

Dust

inside my lungs. coating my legs
my face my clothes my eyes
under my fingernails
thick within my ear canals
in the ridges of my fingerprints
finer than powder
the brown of terminal illness and raging floodwaters
turning my hair into string
my throat into rubber
my skin into chalk
rub your fingers along my arm
watch how it rolls off like black eraser shavings
into your palm

I sift sand through my hands, laughing distractedly
at a throwaway comment. a campfire splutters.
Dust dominates all.
with every story or moment's peace,
it's there

in the air, Dust is different. Dust explodes
over the crowded skylines
and the nauseating empty horizons
the soft pastel gradient
yellow to peach
to murky green to blue
to delicate violet
Dust gives height to the sky and amplifies the sun
it spreads with triumph above everything
it escapes itself and bathes the earth in its own light

I may not belong to this place but my body is here
being converted
cell by cell
into Dust

in moments of doubt

I press my hand against the thin bone of my sternum
and feel my tiny heart beating in fierce determination
in fragile eagerness

so small, so miraculous
I am unworthy to have it in my service
yet grateful that it
never listens to what I tell it

it would be a disservice to deny the tiny animal in my chest

coming alive in new connections and landscapes
sentimental but quick to forget
selfish, so selfish
but always ready to find itself in others

love

you'll meet people who shake you so vividly
recalibrate your very core
so that when you return the skies will look bluer
the native bush more rugged and raw
the clay smell more earthy
when you return home you'll wish they were there
so you could shove the New Zealand-ness
down
their
throats
to prove you're not just making it all up
you'll never see a chalkboard sign
advertising specials on Kumara or taro
or a barefoot barbecue
or bumping into someone on every
single
bus ride in a week
or a pataka kai laden with feijoas and lemons
or a waiata sung at a rugby match

the same way again

you'll always have that so-called foreigner in your head

just waiting for you to ask

"so, what do you think of New Zealand?"

KUMARA
$2.99
KG

NECTARINE
$2.99
KG

the mural in Auckland
international airport
security area

spoiler alert - you'll never find
that sunbleached impossibly green blue white paradise
I think it's government propaganda
to stymie the brain drain
I wonder how many people have run out
of the terminal after seeing that picture
chasing that impossibly beautiful view

grounded

nothing feels like home as much
as the lichen growing in the cracks of the footpath
as you wheel your bag out of the taxi bay
and onto the cracked asphalt of
that first suburban street

facebook

the digital world will sometimes jolt you
unexpectedly from one home to the other
wrenching you with nausea from persona to persona
so don't be afraid to fall behind on the goss
take the time to be present and soak it all in
and remember that dirt is dirt
and air is air
no matter where you are

usurper

home is the people you leave
and despite your best intentions
they move, and change, and tend towards entropy
unsure whose shoulder to tap on
as friend groups steadily disintegrated
swirling drifting chaos
you are part of the process, whether you intended it or not
it may take years or a lifetime to shirk the label of Usurper
even if you spend all of your energy to make up for
lost
time

panic

if you feel our whole world closing in
two hours before your flight
sweating and pacing aimlessly
through overpriced convenience stores
 and banal magazine racks
coiling your phone charger around
and around
your wrist
and you make the mistake of checking
Instagram to witness the highlight reels
of the elusive Kiwi Summer™
you willingly sacrificed (why?)
to dive blindly into the white unknown

and you picked the wrong book
featuring somehow settled twenty-somethings
acting out soapy dramas
and treating their impossibly large friend circles
with such carelessness
and the words blur

and you take one last look at the solemn,

heavy spine of Waitakere ranges,

the David Trubridge lights in the bar

the tired multigenerational families shuffling past

sporting Warrior's jerseys and Canterbury logos

give in

go to McDonalds

(and enjoy your last proper milkshake for a while)

a funeral via video call

at the time, you have it easier
you can swipe away
notifications from ten missed calls
and pretend that life goes on
absence chokes when you return
a grieving that is private, relentless
yours alone

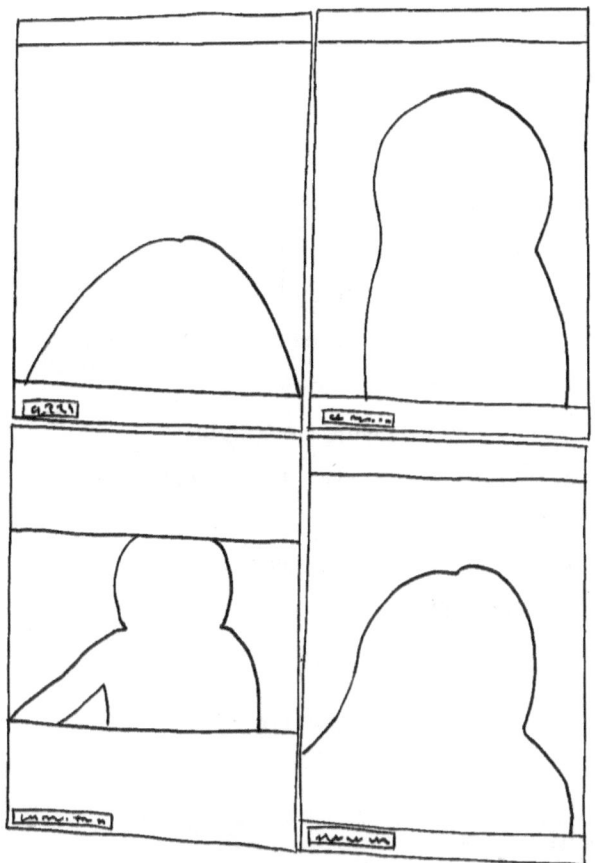

stock your suitcase

the familiar brands stare down from the shelves
at your former local dairy
sickeningly rich milk products
fifty cent lolly bags now at the mercy of inflation
biscuits and muesli bars and
Milo tins and New Zealand Geographics
like the detritus of your grandparents cupboard
late stage capitalism, true
but the shelves stare kindly back at you
like your oldest friend

hollow

it may happen that
in your absence
places empty themselves of the important people
suburbia drained of meaning

and leave only a vaudevillian husk of their former selves
overgrown swing sets
or repainted restaurants
best not to return
than to walk amongst ghosts

special

you may not have thought of our tiny country as that
unique
until you left it
and realised our Waitangi tribunal is somehow
the world's best attempt at indigenous reparation (?)
and that Auckland is the biggest Pasifika city on the
planet
and that conservation isn't usually about killing
anything warm blooded
and that our accents are pretty unusual

you will certainly play it up for your new friends
or sing them the national anthem in Te Reo
with more pride than your usual mumble
it's ok, we all do it
you can admit
only under your breath that
we are actually pretty special

magpie

some places have
buses that arrive on time
affordable trains that cross the country over
brick suburbs made somehow beautiful from their bleak
past
fresh fruit on rotation on crowded beaches
open air bars where everyone knows the same samba moves
traffic delays from wayward troops of baboons
slave castles with unavoidable history of past massacres
baked into the coral concrete
corn syrup American candies which taste consistently stale
boat parties and gold coffees and palm wine and henna
lives louder and quieter than ours
collect your shiny cultural differences

maybe like me you'll love
the seats in an airport

the way your body contorts to fit in them
neck bent over the metal bars
jeans sticking to the black pleather
one eye on the gate, one on your novel
(more likely, your phone)
solid comfort in the hours of temporariness

you'll cry in either direction

the only time I didn't was when I sat next to a Samoan
pastor
and we had the sanest conversation I had in days
no more "see you next year"s or final farewells
he simply listened to me explain
the broad strokes of my aimless travels
I bathed in his effortless mana
and he laughed at my naive musings on cultural differences
and he told me about his home
and we sat in silence
and he blessed me
and then we both left
and I walked down the loading bridge warm
in the knowledge that my parents
and sister
were waiting for me on the other end

Bath and Bodyworks
Cosy Body Lotion

a friend gave it to me during my final months
this body lotion and its delicate faintly tropical fragrance
is liquid memory
it smells of blurry goodbyes and face masks
and futile attempts at soothing sunburn
and panicky drinking and sweeping sand
off of the vinyl floor
I have been using it scarcely
but the colours on the label are fading
and I only have a little left

I see you

but your eyes are elsewhere
you recite words in a language I am hopeless to understand
you orient your body using an app on your phone
and tread with humility
the worn paths of your father's religion
I am lost to you
I try to follow you, to find some hint of the person I know
in the beads you count
the verses you cradle deep within your memory
the gentleness with which
you touch your forehead to the ground
the flicked droplets of water with which you cleanse yourself
after all these many months it seems
I am still blind to your world
I can't get in

I feel like myself around you

through the calculated systemic
gut wrenching
shattering of self
that is the act of moving away
you'll find a funhouse mirror of your character
scattered around the globe

the guy who bolsters your mana
in a way you wished you knew
how to do on your own
your ropu of girls almost mythical
in the cabal of feminine power you create
while alone you all too often
turn feminism into a subconscious competition
the terrifyingly bright stoners and hippies
who remind you of all that ever mattered
music food and earth

who make your struggle to sterilise
and monetise
your naive ideals
seem universal rather than lonely

your whanau
grounding you with dizzying speed
the moment you hear your mum's voice

you become a being of many throbbing hearts
oases which never stay constant
connected by threads and tubes
hold loose, but never let go

I know it's your secret shame

but it's okay to admit
that things may be better across the ditch
cocktails on Bondi beach
surfers with washboard abs and sexy (?) mullets
a wide pool of multicultural young people
more sun, more vitamin D
more competition amongst supermarkets
and suitors

something is a little cheerier
three hours flight from home
maybe it's just
the thirty percent paybump

the important ones

itemised like a shopping list in your notes app
is it enough to dissect myself cleanly
over a half hour coffee
two days before I fly off
again
do you forgive me for making you
the poster girl of Life at Home
I love you
did you hear that? do you feel it?
I love you
I swear I love you
I'll get the cheque

sorry

I wanted to ask her how much it hurt
when I left
and how I can make it up to her
instead I found a little prayer pocket
in her bedside drawer one day
filled with small items and a list of prayers for Katie
it shattered me
the strength of her love

shock

nothing reminds you that the world is actually
impossibly enormous and that we are but
slightly more complicated meat sacks
crawling across its surface
like staring down the beast of nine hour jetlag
back in your childhood home

waking up before others leave and go to work
the sigh of wind and rattle of timber cladding outside
you can try to distract yourself with books or social media
but the finality is relentless, claustrophobic
you are back in New Zealand
this is it

the whorls and knots in the wood of the dresser
the delicately decaying blinds
the seasons garish and bold
obvious from the outrageously festive pohutukawa outside
the sun softer, yes, but still distinct

a nip of cold

do we have an internal clock for seasons too?
if so, will I ever reset mine?

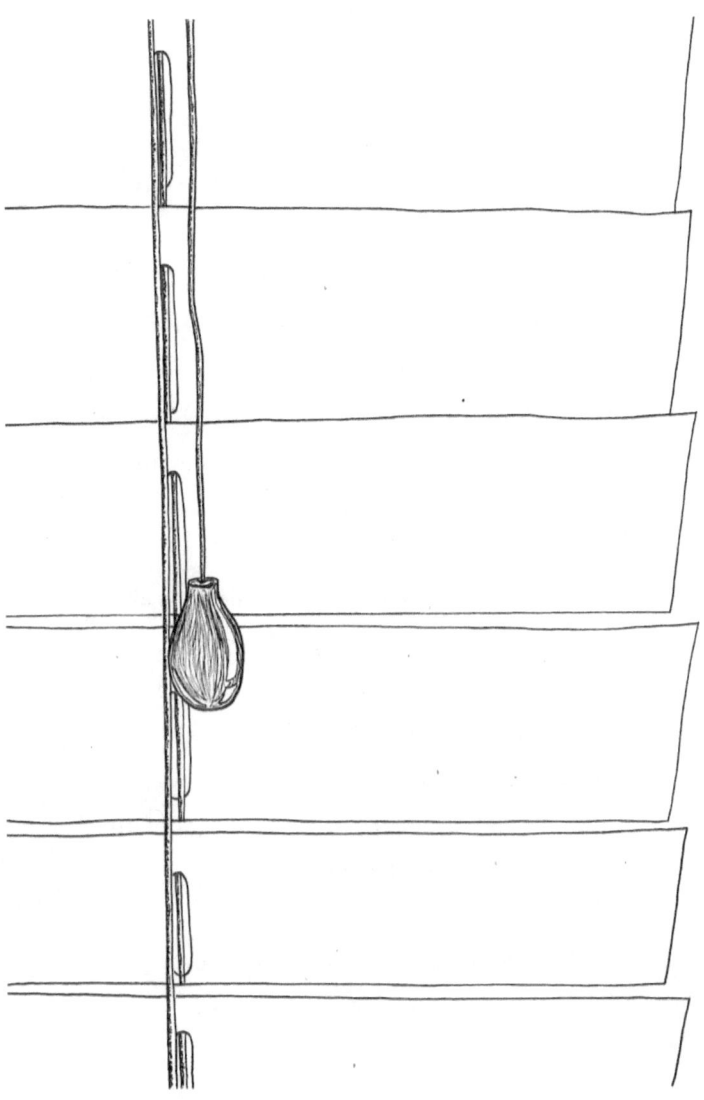

I'm back

you'll wonder
if people can see your discomfort
in your stiffness leaning against the windowsill
in your hesitancy recalling a name
from scouts or rugby
or some past version of you they recognise

can people see you squirm
in hearing sweeping generic statements about
countries or cities where you know the
colour of gum stuck on the sidewalks
layouts of obscure malls and cafes
and the unique sparse foliage
and the billboards for face whitening cream
the avocados the size of babies
and bars where you danced freely
in the turquoise glow of the aquarium
having to nod, not give anything away

reverse culture shock may sound fictitious
but manage the symptoms just in case it's real

patriot

you may find a new sense of "New Zealandness" in yourself
in the way you present yourself to the world

as if by clinging to our particular flavour
of former British colony
you'll find some nugget of truth
of culture, of heart
beyond the outdated plastic iconography of Kiwiana
used to decorate two dollar shop kitsch
and actually not that unique
jandals are the world's most common footwear
tomato sauce is just ketchup trying to be quirky

you may alternative between pride and embarrassment
nostalgia and loneliness
hovering at the outskirts of groups and bars
then being thrust unwillingly into the centre
to defend yourself

you may reach that truth
through hurried and defensive emphasis
on our proud indigenous culture
that was up until now, at most, background noise to your
life

or you may simply end up caring too much about
Jono and Ben or L&P chocolate
or some other piece of cultural detritus
even if not particularly good, they're ours
and you cling to these artifacts like a liferaft
something, anything
to both inadequately explain and complicate
who you are

some days begin as stories
and thus are never lived

the future

through the gap between the airplane seats
through which we often forget we are vulnerable to the
world
and are therefore secret portals into other lives
I saw a woman, her skin Kiwi-leathery-sunspotted
with careful, deliberate pen strokes she wrote
Devan
Sarah
Shriti
first in the small notebook she had placed on her tray table
then on the wrinkled skin of her left hand

ever optimistic, I imagined they were her friends overseas
connections lovingly enshrined after
years and miles of
distance
she was going to send them postcards when we landed
active in memory, alive
a web of aroha tethering her to
all facets of her earth

visiting

a ready made family will feel
incredible
a triumph, a milestone
an invite around a Local Dinner Table

home cooked food in excess
(altered and devoid of spice for the Western pallet, of
course)
like a nervous new boyfriend meeting the parents you'll
lay the charm on thick
like the unfamiliar margarine brand you'll spread
on the warm dinner rolls you'll eat too much of
and hope they don't notice

the conversation will journey in a smooth 360
around the room
as you cluelessly enquire regarding the origins of trophies
decorative plates, cabinets, china

you'll recount your own family story
and be shocked by it, moved by it afresh,
previously unexamined, mundane

you'll certainly feel the dull heavy thud of
your privilege in your chest
but 'playing ladies', being hosted
can even the playing field a little

a ready made family can be a bit like paracetamol
just never tell mum.

I can read the characters, but I can't understand the meaning

I know the bus schedule but have no clue
what the menacing inflatable rats mean
or what that huge clock is counting down to
I can sway awkwardly at the concert but have no idea
why one man glared at me the whole three hours
I can state Salam Alaikum to fellow
motorcyclists with confidence
and blush at my friends confused laughter
(we were in the wrong country for the greeting)
I can become addicted to biscoff spread
on dry wheat crackers for breakfast
but don't understand why I've only ever
encountered it in a backwater Ghanaian supermarket
I can read the characters
but I don't understand the meaning

should you mow your neighbour's lawn?

with a gusto I seem never to channel at home
I organised a beach clean up
collecting rubbish which I deemed
carelessly strewn around the place
shocked at the disrespect
A few of my friends trailed behind me and
though inadequately prepared
we made somewhat of an impact

suddenly, the beach ahead of us was clear of detritus
no plastic, metal, even rocks and seaweed

I found out later that one Emirate hires beach cleaners
one does not
the border just happened to pass right through
the middle of the beach

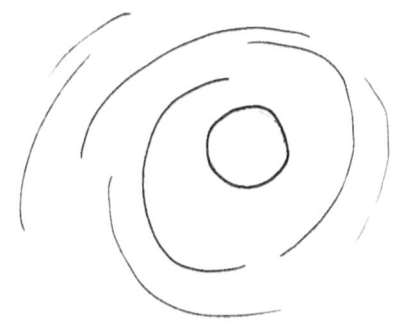

*something difficult will
happen and you will need
to go to the mall*

like sucking on a dummy
you'll crave the fluorescent lights
the sometimes familiar brands
the garish coloured packaging
and the universally fatty food court smell
the big Cs - colonisation, capitalism
turn the world into a homogenous soup
anywhere you go, you will round a corner
to be bombarded with advertisements
ready and waiting
to wash against you and cleanse your spirit
when you let them

grandma

I arrived home and was dedicated to spending time with her
I wasn't going to make the same mistake again
our circular conversations, both of us bedridden
her unwell, me despairing in MIQ
told me this time was precious

I sat on her couch and she asked me
"Katie, was it worth it?"
I knew she was talking about my leaving
it hung like a spectre at that stage
it clung heavy to my neck
I wasn't surprised she could see it

at that moment it was too raw
I choked out a meaningless affirmative
before my voice wavered too much

truthfully

I'm not sure the answer to her question

whether the sum of my

fastidious adherence to the checkboxes of the mythical

'big OE'

add up to anything of meaning in the adult world

but I shall still treat the person I turned into

with respect

and feel like I managed to build a new home

to leave

passport privilege

though I try to stop myself
I will sometimes brandish my worn passport
like an engagement ring
making sure all could see its thickness with visas
the silver fern worn off the spine
leafing through pages and reminiscing
in a very public place
feels so wrong
and yet, so powerful
in a few years, it will be no longer a tool
but a memento

*to fly is to be viscerally
confronted with who you
are*

your place in the world, the water you've been swimming in

quickly, who you are becomes who you were
and with each return you'll contort yourself
into the misshappen cookie cutters of former selves
finally relenting, accepting you're still more at ease
throwing everything to the wind and
starting afresh

more at ease with meeting strangers at hostels
or sleeping on the floor of an airport
than the hard mahi of actually settling in and creating a life
the far greater challenge

trapped

there is no 'right time' to leave
leave too soon, you'll miss out on
the formative social years of university
and have to start from scratch in a fragmented world
of preoccupied young adults

leave with your family, you'll raise second culture kids
'expats' if you're white, 'immigrants' if you're anything else
they'll come home with American accents
following trends all the more impossible to decipher
(and you'll be guilt tripped for fuelling the brain drain
and leaving your aging parents)
leave with an empty nest
you're too old for backpacking culture
and your kids will resent you
for spending their one shot at a house

you'll never find it, that movie moment
when you realise now is the time
that farewell party, a chorus of "Now is the Hour"
sung by your loved ones with more sweetness than
bitterness

but you'll do it
and it will be okay

leaving

throwing your life in disarray
it's a muscle, gradually built
but don't let it get too strong

you are allowed to let love to seep into your life
and it's always hard to say goodbye

About the Author

Katie is a Kiwi and recent 'COVID returnee' who studied at New York University Abu Dhabi, taking classes in New York, Bahrain, Ghana, Djibouti and beyond. She is now a sustainability professional working in the Waikato, and is always saving money for her next trip.